Let's Discover Canada

NEWFOUNDLAND

by
Suzanne LeVert

George Sheppard
McMaster University
General Editor

CHELSEA HOUSE PUBLISHERS

New York   Philadelphia

Cover: Woods Point, Newfoundland
Opposite: A cyclist coasts along near Trout River, a town on Newfoundland's west coast.

Chelsea House Publishers
EDITOR-IN-CHIEF: Remmel Nunn
MANAGING EDITOR: Karyn Gullen Browne
COPY CHIEF: Mark Rifkin
PICTURE EDITOR: Adrian G. Allen
ART DIRECTOR: Maria Epes
ASSISTANT ART DIRECTOR: Noreen Romano
MANUFACTURING MANAGER: Gerald Levine
SYSTEMS MANAGER: Lindsey Ottman
PRODUCTION MANAGER: Joseph Romano
PRODUCTION COORDINATOR: Marie Claire Cebrián

Let's Discover Canada
SENIOR EDITOR: Rebecca Stefoff

Staff for NEWFOUNDLAND
COPY EDITOR: Benson D. Simmonds
EDITORIAL ASSISTANT: Ian Wilker
PICTURE RESEARCHER: Wendy Wills
DESIGNER: Diana Blume

First Printing

1   3   5   7   9   8   6   4   2

Library of Congress Cataloging-in-Publication Data
LeVert, Suzanne.
    Let's discover Canada. Newfoundland/by Suzanne LeVert; George Sheppard, general editor.
        p.   cm.
    Includes bibliographical references and index.
    Summary: Illustrated text explores the history, geography, and culture of Newfoundland.
    ISBN 0-7910-1027-9
    1. Newfoundland—Juvenile literature.   [1. Newfoundland.]
    I. Sheppard, George C. B.   II. Title.
    F1122.4.L48   1991   90-46040
    971.8—dc20   CIP
                                                                                                 AC

Contents

My Canada

by Pierre Berton

"Nobody knows my country," a great Canadian journalist, Bruce Hutchison, wrote almost half a century ago. It is still true. Most Americans, I think, see Canada as a pleasant vacationland and not much more. And yet we are the United States's greatest single commercial customer, and the United States is our largest customer.

Lacking a major movie industry, we have made no wide-screen epics to chronicle our triumphs and our tragedies. But then there has been little blood in our colonial past—no revolutions, no civil war, not even a wild west. Yet our history is crammed with remarkable men and women. I am thinking of Joshua Slocum, the first man to sail alone around the world, and Robert Henderson, the prospector who helped start the Klondike gold rush. I am thinking of some of our famous artists and writers—comedian Dan Aykroyd, novelists Margaret Atwood and Robertson Davies, such popular performers as Michael J. Fox, Anne Murray, Gordon Lightfoot, and k.d. lang, and hockey greats from Maurice Richard to Gordie Howe to Wayne Gretzky.

The real shape of Canada explains why our greatest epic has been the building of the Pacific Railway to unite the nation from

sea to sea in 1885. On the map, the country looks square. But because the overwhelming majority of Canadians live within 100 miles (160 kilometers) of the U.S. border, in practical terms the nation is long and skinny. We are in fact an archipelago of population islands separated by implacable barriers—the angry ocean, three mountain walls, and the Canadian Shield, that vast desert of billion-year-old rock that sprawls over half the country, rich in mineral treasures, impossible for agriculture.

Canada's geography makes the country difficult to govern and explains our obsession with transportation and communication. The government has to be as involved in railways, airlines, and broadcasting networks as it is with social services such as universal medical care. Rugged individualism is not a Canadian quality. Given the environment, people long ago learned to work together for security.

It is ironic that the very bulwarks that separate us—the chiseled peaks of the Selkirk Mountains, the gnarled scarps north of Lake Superior, the ice-choked waters of the Northumberland Strait —should also be among our greatest attractions for tourists and artists. But if that is the paradox of Canada, it is also the glory.

Newfoundland's Gros Morne National Park—a wilderness of woodlands, moors, and rugged coastal cliffs—epitomizes the austere beauty of Canada's easternmost province.

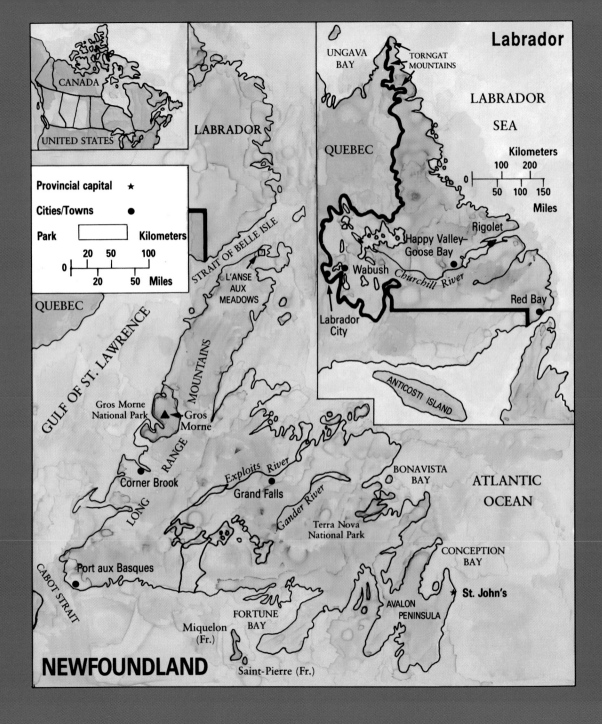

CANADA

UNITED STATES

LABRADOR

Provincial capital ★

Cities/Towns ●

Park ☐   Kilometers

0 20 50 100

20 50 Miles

QUEBEC

GULF OF ST. LAWRENCE

STRAIT OF BELLE ISLE

L'ANSE
AUX
MEADOWS

LONG RANGE MOUNTAINS

Gros Morne
National Park ▲ ← Gros
Morne

Corner Brook ●

Exploits River

Grand Falls ●

Gander River

Terra Nova
National Park

BONAVISTA
BAY

ATLANTIC
OCEAN

CONCEPTION
BAY

Port aux Basques ●

CABOT STRAIT

FORTUNE
BAY

Miquelon
(Fr.)

Saint-Pierre (Fr.)

AVALON
PENINSULA

St. John's ★

NEWFOUNDLAND

Labrador

UNGAVA
BAY

TORNGAT
MOUNTAINS

LABRADOR

SEA

QUEBEC

Kilometers

100 200

0

50 100 150

Miles

Rigolet ●

Happy Valley–
Goose Bay ●

Wabush ●   Churchill River

Labrador
City

Red Bay ●

ANTICOSTI ISLAND

Pitcher plant

Puffin

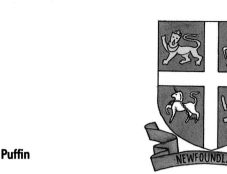

NEWFOUNDLAND

Newfoundland at a Glance

Area: 156,185 square miles (404,519 square kilometers)

Population: 568,349 (1986 census)

Capital: St. John's (population 96,216)

Other cities: Corner Brook (population 22,719), Labrador City (population 8,664), Happy Valley–Goose Bay (population 7,248)

Major rivers: Churchill, Exploits

Principal products: Fish, forestry products, iron ore, hydroelectric power

Entered Dominion of Canada: March 31, 1949

Motto: *Quaerite prime regnum dei* (Seek ye first the Kingdom of God)

Provincial coat of arms: Red shield with white cross, two lions to represent England, and two unicorns to represent Scotland, with Native Canadians on either side and an elk on top of the shield; created in 1637, adopted in 1928

Provincial flag: Red, white, and blue design based upon the Union Jack, the flag of Great Britain; adopted in 1980

Government: Parliamentary system with a single-chambered legislature; 52 legislative representatives are popularly elected by district for terms of 5 years; the formal head of state is the lieutenant governor, appointed by Canada's federal government as representative of the British Crown; the head of government is the premier, leader of the dominant political party; the premier appoints an executive council from the legislative assembly; Newfoundland is represented in the federal government in Ottawa by 6 senators and 7 members of the House of Commons

The Land

Perhaps more than any other province in Canada, Newfoundland is defined by its relationship with the sea. The province consists of two parts, the island of Newfoundland and the region called Labrador on the Canadian mainland. The two are separated by a channel called the Strait of Belle Isle, and both the island and Labrador have long, rugged seacoasts. The fishing grounds that surround the island—among the most productive in the world— have shaped the province's history and economy.

Newfoundland is the largest of Canada's four Atlantic provinces; the others are Prince Edward Island, Nova Scotia, and New Brunswick. Although larger than the other three Atlantic provinces combined, Newfoundland accounts for little more than four percent of Canada's total land area. It is the seventh largest Canadian province in area and the ninth largest in population. Its overall area is 156,185 square miles (404,519 square kilometers). Mainland Labrador, with an area of 112,826 square miles (292,219 square kilometers), is more than two and one half times as large as the island of Newfoundland, which has an area of 43,359 square miles (112,300 square kilometers).

Opposite: Cape St. Mary's, on the Avalon Peninsula of Newfoundland island, is a bird sanctuary. Each spring and summer, thousands of gannets and murres nest on narrow ledges above the sea.
Above: Labrador, Newfoundland's mainland territory, is a vast expanse of bleak, rocky terrain, sparsely populated but rich in mineral resources.

Labrador is a roughly triangular wedge on the eastern coast of mainland Canada. On the west and south it is bordered by the province of Quebec. The Atlantic Ocean is on the southeast; on the northeast is the Labrador Sea, which lies between Labrador and the Danish-owned island of Greenland. Newfoundland island is situated at the mouth of the Gulf of St. Lawrence, 10 to 20 miles (16 to 32 kilometers) from Labrador across the Strait of Belle Isle. The southwestern tip of the island is separated from the province of Nova Scotia by the 68-mile-wide (109-kilometer-wide) Cabot Strait.

As the easternmost province in Canada, Newfoundland is closer to Europe than to many points in North America. For example, the capital city of St. John's is closer to Ireland than it is to the city of Winnipeg in central Canada. Except for the eastern edge of Greenland, Newfoundland is the easternmost part of North America. Because it is so far east, Newfoundland has its own time zone—30 minutes ahead of the rest of Atlantic Canada.

Rockbound Landscapes

Newfoundland and Labrador are beautiful, but theirs is a stern, uncompromising beauty. The French navigator Jacques Cartier, one of the first Europeans to explore the region, described the coast of Labrador as "stones and frightful rocks and uneven places," and said, "On this entire coast I saw not one cartload of earth, though I landed in many places." On both the island and the mainland, the terrain is indeed rocky and rather desolate. There are no grand mountain peaks, only endless vistas of blunt crags and bluffs, hills and valleys covered with Arctic spruce and tundra, and thousands of lakes and streams. The province's highest point is in the Torngat Mountains in the far north of Labrador. These jagged mountains, eroded over the centuries by rivers and glaciers into a fringe of winding fjords, reach heights of 5,500 feet (1,667 meters). The highest point on the island of Newfoundland is a 2,672-foot (810-meter) peak called Gros Morne in the Long Range Mountains, near the city of Corner Brook.

Near Red Bay, Labrador, the Pinware River rushes through a spruce forest. Farther north, the forest gives way to open tundra.

Thousands of years ago, glaciers scraped away most of the soil from Labrador and Newfoundland, leaving the land barren and stony, so much so that Newfoundland has been nicknamed the Rock. But this rocky terrain contains a wealth of mineral resources. Western Labrador has some of the most extensive iron ore deposits in North America.

Although soil suitable for agriculture is scarce in Newfoundland, the province has large forests of evergreen trees, which can grow in shallow, rocky soil. More than 60 percent of Newfoundland island is forested with black spruce, balsam fir, and red and white pine. Labrador, too, has some dense forests of tall evergreens, mostly in the river valleys. But approximately half of Labrador is covered by lichen forests, which consist of slow-growing black spruce, somewhat stunted but hardy enough to survive the region's long winters and short growing seasons, with carpets of lichens and mosses between the trees. The northern part of Labrador is frigid, treeless tundra, where only mosses and occasional dwarf willow and alder shrubs can grow.

The coastlines of both the island and the mainland are greatly indented by many bays and fjords. The island's southeast coast consists of a series of deep bays and coves alternating with

A herd of caribou moves across the grassland of the Avalon Peninsula. Threatened by overhunting during the 19th and early 20th centuries, Newfoundland's two species of caribou have made a comeback in recent decades.

steep headlands and rugged peninsulas. Avalon Peninsula, where the capital is located, is almost an island itself, connected to the rest of Newfoundland by only a narrow neck of land. Fortune Bay, west of Avalon Peninsula, has some of Newfoundland's most dramatic landscapes, with sheer cliffs that rise 590 to 984 feet (180 to 300 meters) from the sea.

Water and Wildlife

As much as one-fifth of the province of Newfoundland is covered with fresh water. Both island and mainland have thousands of lakes, ponds, streams, and bogs. Many are tiny, but some are quite large and deep. The Smallwood Reservoir in Labrador, for instance, covers approximately 2,500 square miles (6,475 square kilometers) and is the tenth largest freshwater body in Canada.

Newfoundland also has powerful rivers. The Exploits is the longest river on the island, coursing 153 miles (245 kilometers) from Red Indian Lake into Notre Dame Bay on the northeast coast. The Gander is another principal river on the island, with a length of about 109 miles (174 kilometers). Named for the many geese that nest along its shores, the Gander was an important waterway for the island's early European settlers and Natives.

The most powerful of the province's waterways is the Churchill River in Labrador. It runs for 532 turbulent miles (856 kilometers) from Ashuanipi Lake and empties into the Atlantic Ocean near the tiny town of Rigolet, plunging over a 222-foot (75-meter) waterfall on the way. Most of the province's hydroelectric plants are located along the Churchill. Experts believe that the Churchill has the potential to produce more hydroelectric power than any other river in North America.

Newfoundland has another water-related energy resource—peat bogs. Peat is an organic material composed of moss, aquatic grasses, and other plants. In wet, low-lying areas, these plants are periodically covered with water, which causes them to decay, and over time the plant matter is compacted into a dense, spongy substance. When dug out of the bog and dried, peat can be burned like coal to provide heat and energy. Peat is harvested in Newfoundland and elsewhere in Canada, and it is usually cut into bricks or slabs. Once regarded as an old-fashioned or primitive fuel, peat has come to be more highly valued in recent years as an energy resource.

Peat bogs hold more than potential energy. They are also the home of Newfoundland's provincial flower, the pitcher plant. This tube-shaped flower is a meat eater. It produces nectar that attracts insects—the bogs are home to untold millions of mosquitoes and other insects. The hapless victims enter the flower in search of nectar, but the flower is lined with downward-pointing bristles from which the insects are unable to escape. They drown in a pool of nectar and water at the bottom of the flower, and the pitcher plant digests them.

Almost 60 species of mammals are native to Newfoundland and Labrador. The province has two species of caribou, woodland and barren ground. The woodland caribou number about 40,000 and live on the island; the barren ground caribou number about 700,000 and live in northern Labrador. For centuries, caribou have been a vital resource for the Native peoples of the region, who hunt them for food and skins. Beginning in the 19th century, however, the caribou were slaughtered in great numbers by white hunters. Since the 1930s,

The province's coasts are clogged with pack ice and icebergs during the long, bitter northern winters. In spring, when the ice fields of the northern waters break up, bergs can be seen drifting south past Labrador and Newfoundland.

they have been protected by strict conservation laws. The hunting of caribou, though still permitted, is limited. The caribou population has increased in recent decades, and large herds of these majestic, antlered creatures once again roam across the northern wilderness. Moose, black bear, beaver, lynx, otter, and red fox are also native to the province.

More than 300 species of birds either live in or migrate through Newfoundland. The coastal cliffs and offshore islands are thronged with crowded colonies of seabirds, especially gulls, gannets, and razor-billed auks. Newfoundland is the major breeding center for the Atlantic puffin, a plump black-and-white seabird with a large red-and-gray bill, which has been named the provincial bird. The island's south coast contains what is probably North America's greatest concentration of bald eagles.

Newfoundland is also known for two breeds of dog that originated on the island—Labrador retrievers and Newfound-

Fogs are common, especially in spring and summer. The heavy condensation caused when cold currents from the north meet warmer waters near Newfoundland makes the province one of the foggiest regions in the world.

lands. Newfoundlands are large dogs, averaging 28 inches (70 centimeters) in height and 150 pounds (69 kilograms) in weight. Newfs, as they are called, have thick, shaggy coats, usually black but sometimes gray or bronze. They are excellent swimmers and are patient and even-tempered. Newfs have been trained to rescue drowning victims. Labrador retrievers are also large dogs, but they have shorter, sleeker coats. Generally either black or pale yellow, Labs originated as sporting dogs, used by hunters to retrieve fallen birds from water. Like Newfs, they are good swimmers.

Climate and Weather

Because the province of Newfoundland stretches for nearly 750 miles (1,200 kilometers) from north to south and has both coastal and interior regions, it has a varied climate. The northern and western parts of Labrador are situated in the subarctic zone, where winter temperatures can reach -50 degrees Fahrenheit (-45.6 degrees Celsius). Even midsummer is cool in this region, with July highs reaching 50° or 60°F (10° or 15°C).

Southern and coastal Labrador and Newfoundland island have a milder climate. Winter temperatures in St. John's, the capital, hover around 15° to 25°F ($-9°$ to $-4°$C). Summer on the island, though brief, is quite lovely. Ocean breezes keep the air crisp and clean, and average high temperatures range from 50° to 60° F (10° to 15°C), although some days are much hotter. Throughout much of the year, the coastal region is shrouded by frequent fogs, which occur when cold air from the interior meets warmer air from the sea.

The History

In 1961, a team of Norwegian archaeologists made one of the most important discoveries in Newfoundland's history: They found the remains of an ancient Viking settlement at l'Anse aux Meadows on the northern peninsula of the island. The findings confirmed that Norse adventurers had found their way across the Atlantic to Newfoundland as early as A.D. 1000. They are now thought to have been the first Europeans ever to see North America.

Norse legends recount that centuries ago certain Vikings sailed from the Norse colonies in Iceland and Greenland to lands farther west. One saga told of Bjarni Herjolfsson, a Viking who was blown off course while sailing from Iceland to Greenland in about A.D. 985. When he finally arrived in Greenland, he spoke of three new lands he had seen in the west. One was forested and hilly, another was forested and flat, and the third was rocky and mountainous. Scholars believe that Herjolfsson had sighted the coasts of Newfoundland, Labrador, and Baffin Island.

Vikings were the first Europeans to visit the shores of Newfoundland. Archaeologists working at L'Anse aux Meadows (above), have uncovered an early Norse settlement that was built around A.D. 1000. The first Viking captain to lead his men ashore in Newfoundland was Leif Eriksson (opposite), the forerunner of European explorers in the New World.

Leif Eriksson was one of the Vikings in Greenland who heard Herjolfsson's story. A dozen years later, Eriksson bought Herjolfsson's ship and went in search of the western lands that Herjolfsson had described. Eriksson and his men landed in three places, which they called Helluland (Rocky Land), Markland (Wooded Land), and Vinland (Wine Land, meaning that it had fruit). Historians now believe that these three landings correspond to the east coast of Labrador, the northern coast of Newfoundland island, and a warm, sheltered bay either on the southern coast of Newfoundland or on Cape Breton Island, Nova Scotia. The Vikings spent the winter in Vinland and returned to Greenland the following spring.

Later, other Norse expeditions visited the new western territory. A few settlements were established in Vinland, including the l'Anse aux Meadows site in Newfoundland, but the settlements were abandoned after attacks by the local Natives, whom the Norse called *skraellings*. The Norse colony in Greenland died out in the 14th century, and knowledge of Vinland and other areas that the Vikings had visited in North America was limited to sagas and legends.

The Natives

The Vikings did not discover an uninhabited new world. A variety of Native Americans had lived in Labrador and on Newfoundland island for centuries. A tribe who called themselves the Mushuau Innu (Barren Land People) lived in central Labrador and northern Newfoundland. Referred to as the Montagnais-Naskapi by Europeans, these Natives were nomadic hunters of caribou and other mammals. They were adept at traveling across their expansive hunting grounds, using canoes during the summer and snowshoes and toboggans during the winter. When the Europeans came to the region in the 15th and 16th centuries, the Innu helped them to start the fur trade that would eventually spread into most of present-day Canada.

North of the Innu lived the Inuit, who were called Eskimos by the southern tribes. The Inuit lived in small communities

A young woman named Shawnandithet was the last known survivor of the Beothuk, one of the Native peoples of Newfoundland. She died in St. John's in 1829. The Beothuk were wiped out by European aggression, intertribal fighting, and starvation.

scattered throughout the Arctic from Alaska to Greenland, including northern Labrador. They were hunters and gatherers who moved seasonally from one camp to another. They spoke a language known as Inuktitut, which is still spoken by many of the more than 25,000 Inuit who live in Canada today.

The Dorset were another Native people living in Newfoundland at the time of the Viking expeditions. Descended from an ancient Arctic culture, the Dorset lived on Newfoundland island from about 500 B.C. until about A.D. 1500. Distantly related to the Inuit, the Dorset lived in houses built of snow and turf. They hunted sea mammals such as the walrus and the narwhal, an Arctic whale.

The interior and the southern coast of Newfoundland were inhabited by the Micmac. This Native group lived in villages all along the east coast of North America, from Massachusetts to Quebec. The Micmac outnumbered the other Native peoples in Newfoundland, and they helped the European settlers survive

John Cabot, an Italian navigator sailing on behalf of King Henry VII of England, made two voyages to Newfoundland and Labrador in the late 15th century, looking—unsuccessfully—for the fabled Northwest Passage.

their first hard winters in the New World. Several thousand Micmac still live in Newfoundland; other Micmac live throughout Atlantic Canada.

The Beothuk people lived on the southern and northeastern coasts of the island. They may well have been the first Natives encountered by Europeans in North America; historians now believe that the *skraellings* who fought with the Vikings were either Beothuk or Dorset fishermen. The Beothuk painted their faces with red dye for certain ceremonies, and some scholars have suggested that *redskin,* a term once used for Native Americans, may have referred to this custom. The Beothuk lived in tents covered with bark or animal skin, and they used bows and arrows for hunting and harpoons for fishing. They numbered about 2,000 when English and French settlers began arriving in the 17th and 18th centuries.

The Beothuk were gradually pushed inland by European fishermen who set up camps on the coast, taking over what had once been the Beothuk fishing grounds. In addition, conflicts with the more aggressive Micmac began to threaten the Beothuk people. Many of them fled the island for the less hospitable shores of Labrador. Sadly, by the early 19th century, the Beothuk people had died out entirely. Some were undoubtedly killed by Europeans and other Natives. Some died of European-introduced diseases, such as tuberculosis and smallpox, against which they had no immunity. Others simply starved to death in the barren regions to which they had been forced to flee. The last surviving Beothuk was a young woman named Shawnandithet, who was captured by English settlers in 1823. Although on the verge of death from starvation, Shawnandithet was able to communicate to her captors an account of the suffering her people had undergone. Her legacy is one of the few clues to the fate of this mysterious people. She died in 1829.

The European Fishery

During the 14th century, fishermen from Portugal and England made regular visits to the Grand Banks, a rich fishing region not far from Newfoundland. It was generally known that there were islands on the other side of these fishing grounds, but it was not until the end of the 15th century, in 1497, that an official expedition of discovery was launched from Europe. The expedition's captain was John Cabot, an Italian navigator employed by King Henry VII of England to find the hoped-for Northwest Passage, the sea route that was believed to link the North Atlantic Ocean with Asia.

Cabot failed to discover this elusive northern water route to the Orient, because no such route exists south of the Arctic Ocean. But he did land at what is now St. John's, in Newfoundland. In 1501, a Portuguese explorer named Gaspar Côrte-Real made a somewhat more thorough exploration, naming several of Newfoundland's bays and capes. In 1534–35, French

By the end of the 16th century, the seasonal cod-fishing industry was well established in Newfoundland. Fishermen from many nations fished in the island's waters and cured their catch on the shores of its sheltered bays.

explorer Jacques Cartier sailed through the Cabot Strait and the Strait of Belle Isle, proving that Newfoundland was indeed an island.

By the middle of the 16th century, dozens of fishing boats from England, France, Spain, and Portugal were arriving in Newfoundland waters every summer. The men would haul in huge catches of cod and then set up camps ashore to split, salt, and sun dry the fish. One group of particularly expert fishermen and sailors came from the southeastern corner of Europe's Bay of Biscay, where France and Spain meet. Known as Basques, these hardy seafarers engaged in whaling in the icy waters between Greenland and Canada. Sometime in the 16th century, Basque seamen founded a whaling station at what is now Red Bay, on the southern coast of Labrador. In the 1980s, archaeologists began uncovering the history of this community.

As the end of the 16th century approached, the fragile spirit of cooperation among the fishermen of different nations in Newfoundland's waters began to wear thin. England, greedy for territory and power, sent Sir Humphrey Gilbert to establish a formal claim to Newfoundland. He landed at the port of St.

The Strait of Belle Isle and the coasts of Labrador and Newfoundland were charted in 1766 by Captain James Cook, a British naval officer who later gained fame for his voyages in the Pacific Ocean.

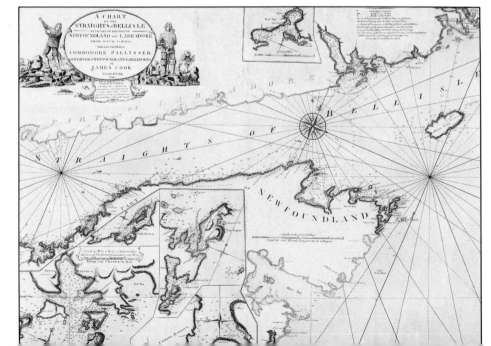

John's on August 3, 1583, and, despite the fact that the harbor was full of ships from Portugal and Spain, he claimed the island for England. The fishermen apparently raised no objection, and Gilbert left a few weeks later. On the way home to England, his ship and crew were lost.

In 1610, King James I of England granted a charter to a group of merchants from the west coast of England. The charter permitted them to establish colonies on the island of Newfoundland, especially on the Avalon Peninsula. The West Country Merchants, as they were called, also received exclusive rights to Newfoundland's offshore fishing grounds.

The merchants' charter caused the development of the Newfoundland colony to lag far behind that of other New World settlements. The West Country Merchants did not want permanent settlers in Newfoundland because such settlers might encroach upon the fishing grounds and compete with their highly profitable seasonal fishing fleets. The merchants went to great lengths to keep settlers out, and they even persuaded the British government to forbid permanent settlement in Newfoundland.

From time to time, however, the Crown did allow communities to be established on the island. The first official colonists, a group of about 40 people, arrived in 1610 with their leader, John Guy. Guy's settlers built a farm, a sawmill, and a stockade in a community they called Cupers Cove (now Cupids Cove) on Conception Bay on the east coast of the Avalon Peninsula. Other settlements followed, but all were threatened by the West Country Merchants.

At the same time, the fishermen had problems of their own: Pirates attacked their boats and looted their stores of fish, supplies, and money. One of the most celebrated pirates in Canadian history was an Englishman named Peter Easton. He led a series of raids against ships from all nations off the coast of Newfoundland, damaging the boats and terrorizing the fishermen.

Starting in 1634, the British government tried to establish law and order in the increasingly rowdy and violent Newfoundland ports. A system called the fishing admiralty was developed. The captain of the first ship to arrive in a

Newfoundland port at the beginning of each summer was named the fishing admiral, or acting governor, for that season. The fishing admiral completely controlled the ships, supplies, and men connected with the fishery. Like the West Country Merchants, the fishing admirals wanted to discourage settlement, and the conflict between the admirals' men and the would-be settlers was bitter and often violent. Houses were burned, and some settlers were beaten or even killed. For a century and a half, the ban on permanent settlement made it very difficult for colonists to clear coastal land for farms and towns. Nevertheless, family holdings and even tiny communities took root in the more remote bays and inlets. Most of these hidden settlements could be reached only by boat. Their inhabitants were called the lost men because they were almost completely cut off from the rest of the world.

The French and the British

The British were not alone in their desire to control Newfoundland's resources. The Spanish and the Portuguese lost their claims in northern North America by the end of the 16th century, but the French were more tenacious. Newfoundland and the rest of Atlantic Canada became part of a long struggle between France and Britain for control of the New World and for economic supremacy in Europe. By the end of the 17th century, the festering European war had reached the New World, and Newfoundland became a bloody battleground.

For nearly 10 years, battles raged between French and British soldiers and ships. Although the French seemed to have the upper hand in Newfoundland, they fared poorly in Europe and finally conceded defeat. The Treaty of Utrecht, signed in 1713, forced France to give up most of its territory in the New World, including all claims in Newfoundland except for fishing privileges along one stretch of coast. The French Shore, as this region was called, stretched from Cape Bonavista on the east coast around the northern tip of the island and partway down the west coast. Seasonal fishermen from France were the only people allowed on this part of the island, and no permanent settlement—French or British—took place there until 1904.

However, the Treaty of Utrecht did not end the dispute between the French and the British. Decades later, during the Seven Years' War (1756–63), Newfoundland was once again a bone of contention between the two nations. In 1762, St. John's was lost and then recaptured by the British. The war between the two European powers ended in 1763 with a British victory, and the final battle was fought on Newfoundland soil.

Although the French were soundly defeated, France kept its rights to the French Shore. In addition, Saint Pierre and Miquelon, two small islands south of Newfoundland, were given to the French. They remain part of France today.

Northern and central Labrador were almost unknown until the 20th century. This early photograph of a snow hut in the winter landscape near Nain, on the north coast, shows the travelers' dogsled. Sleds are still used in the north, although they have been largely replaced by snowmobiles.

Settlement

A few small settlements were established in Newfoundland during the 18th century. The rate of settlement increased slightly after 1729, when the British crown—disturbed by complaints about the brutality of the fishing admirals—appointed a naval officer as governor of the island. In 1763, at the close of the Seven Years' War, 12,000 people inhabited the island and the southern

Labrador shore. After the war, English and Irish colonists arrived to develop and settle the Rock, as Newfoundland soon came to be known. A great wave of immigration occurred during the early part of the 19th century, especially after 1811, when the British government made it legal for colonists to own land and build homes. By 1827, the population had risen to more than 60,000.

As the population increased, so did the demands for better government and local representation. After many months of negotiations with local officials, the British crown granted Newfoundland representative government in 1832. This allowed the colonists to elect an assembly from within their own communities. Most of the real power, however, remained in the hands of a Crown-appointed legislative council. This changed in 1855, when Newfoundland was granted full colonial status, and the power of the elected assembly was greatly increased.

In 1867, some of the other British colonies in North America joined to form a union. This act of confederation resulted in the creation of the Dominion of Canada, an independent country within the British Commonwealth. The founding members of the Confederation were Canada West (Ontario), Canada East (Quebec), New Brunswick, and Nova Scotia. Newfoundlanders

The St. John's fire of 1892 swept through the tightly packed rows of wooden buildings and left much of the city in blackened ruins. Newfoundlanders at once began rebuilding their capital.

decided against joining the Confederation, because they felt much closer to Great Britain—both geographically and in terms of their national and cultural heritage—than to the rest of Canada. This pro-British spirit endures among many Newfoundlanders today. In addition, the people of Newfoundland could see no compelling economic reasons to join the Confederation. They believed that Newfoundland could rely on its own natural resources and was unlikely to receive much help from the Dominion of Canada.

By the latter part of the 19th century, Newfoundland's salt cod industry was still thriving, pulp-and-paper mills were in operation at Grand Falls, and iron ore mines had opened on Bell Island in Conception Bay. Seal hunters had begun taking huge numbers of fur seals from the ice north of Newfoundland, adding a profitable new industry to the island's economy, while farmers had begun harvesting potatoes. Construction of the island's extensive railway network, begun in 1881, opened up the interior to settlement. By the end of the 19th century, more than 200,000 people lived in the colony of Newfoundland.

The 20th Century

In spite of its natural resources, Newfoundland was unable to develop a strong and stable economy. Its main industry, the fishery, was particularly vulnerable to changes in the worldwide demand for cod. When this demand declined, as it often did, the value of the colony's fish harvests declined as well. Almost all food had to be imported from Europe or from other parts of North America, often at great cost. Furthermore, the new railroads, mines, and mills were built with borrowed money, and the colony was sinking deeply into debt.

Newfoundland's economy was devastated by World War I (1914–18), which almost completely halted the fishing industry. The colony, however, made a tremendous contribution to the war effort: More than 6,000 of its young men volunteered to fight on the battlefields of Europe. More than 1,000 men from Newfoundland were killed in the war, and almost 2,500 others were wounded.

Newfoundland's H Company musters recruits for World War I. In support of Great Britain, the colony sent a great many soldiers, sailors, and airmen to fight in both world wars.

After the war, in recognition of Newfoundland's gallant contribution, Great Britain began to treat Newfoundland as an independent dominion, like Canada or Australia. This status was confirmed by the Statute of Westminster in 1931 and, as a result, Newfoundland actually became an independent country. Unfortunately, independence did not guarantee economic success. The burden of debt caused by the war and the earlier expenses of the railroad construction took a toll on Newfoundland's economy. When the world economy collapsed during the Great Depression of the 1930s, Newfoundland could no longer pay its bills. Turning to Great Britain for assistance, Newfoundland temporarily suspended self-government and became, once again, a British colony in 1934. It was administered by a commission consisting of a governor and six commissioners appointed by the Crown. The commission established programs to improve health care, education, and employment conditions in the colony.

In the meantime, Labrador had been added to the colony. Ownership of the sparsely populated eastern end of the great Labrador-Ungava peninsula had been disputed for many years: The Canadian colony of Quebec claimed the territory, and so did British-controlled Newfoundland. In 1927, a judicial committee in Great Britain ruled that the Labrador coast region did belong to Newfoundland, under the terms of the 1763 Treaty of Paris. Canada accepted the ruling, and the present boundary between Newfoundland's Labrador territory and Quebec was established.

When World War II (1939–45) broke out in Europe and Asia, Newfoundland was once again ready to make a significant contribution. Thousands of Newfoundlanders served overseas as soldiers, sailors, and airmen, but this time, however, the war also came to Newfoundland. German submarines cruised Newfoundland's waters and torpedoed Bell Island and St. John's, sinking hundreds of ships off the coast. Yet in many ways the war was a boon to the colony. During the war, Newfoundland enjoyed full employment, and its natural resources, including fish, iron ore, and timber, were in great demand. In addition, the United States, Canada, and Britain built several army bases, two large naval bases, and five airports on the island and in Labrador. The money paid to lease these bases was a much-needed boost to the colony's economy. By the end of the war, the administrative commission was able to pay all of Newfoundland's debts and had a surplus of nearly $40 million.

In 1946, the people of Newfoundland faced the task of setting a course for their future. They had three choices: to return to independent dominion status, to remain a British colony administered by the commission, or to join the Canadian Confederation. A referendum was called so that each Newfoundlander could vote on the issue.

One politician who urged the colony to join the Confederation was Joseph R. Smallwood, a dynamic and controversial man who would remain at the forefront of Newfoundland politics for more than two decades. Smallwood wanted Newfoundland to unite with Canada, claiming that "under confederation we would be better off in pocket, in stomach, and in health." Indeed, in the 1940s Canada was a stable, thriving nation that could offer Newfoundland considerable economic support. Funds from Canada's federal government could help build new roads and could sustain families during seasonal slumps in the fishing and forestry industries. And it seemed logical to Smallwood and many other

Joseph R. Smallwood signs the document that made Newfoundland part of Canada. After Newfoundland joined the Confederation in 1949, Smallwood became the province's first premier.

Newfoundlanders that they should become part of the much larger neighboring country that was so willing to offer them assistance.

On July 22, 1948, the people of Newfoundland voted on the colony's future. By a margin of just four percent, one of Britain's oldest colonies became Canada's newest province. Canada accepted Newfoundland into the Confederation at midnight on March 31, 1949. At the same time, Smallwood became premier of Newfoundland's first provincial government. He held this position until 1972.

Due to an enormous influx of federal money, Newfoundland prospered during the first three decades after Confederation. The fishing industry was modernized, more pulp-and-paper mills were built, and the mineral resources of the island were mined. During the 1950s, the huge iron ore mines of western Labrador came into production as well. But manufacturing, high technology, and financial services—the staples of most modern economies—were severely neglected in Newfoundland.

The economic progress that followed Confederation was to a great extent undermined during the economic recession of the late 1970s and early 1980s. At the beginning of the 1990s, Newfoundland is more dependent than ever on the federal government for support. The province's unemployment rate is high—17 percent—and Newfoundland has the lowest income per person of any province in Canada. Each year, more than 5,000 young people, facing the bleak prospects of building a future in Newfoundland, leave the province to seek work elsewhere.

In addition to its deep-rooted economic problems, Newfoundland is embroiled in two disputes concerning the profits from its natural resources. One of these disputes involves Quebec. Although the courts have awarded Labrador to Newfoundland, Quebec has managed to garner the profits from one of Labrador's most important resources—the hydroelectric power from the Churchill Falls plant. Newfoundland borrowed money from Quebec to build the plant, and in return Newfoundland signed a 40-year agreement to sell the energy produced by the plant to Quebec for a small fraction of its market value. Quebec has been

Clyde Wells, Newfoundland's premier in 1990, discusses the Meech Lake Accord, a proposed amendment to Canada's constitution that would have given special status to Quebec and its French-speaking population. Along with the province of Manitoba, Newfoundland opposed the passage of the accord, which failed to become law.

selling electricity to residents of Canada or the United States and reaping huge profits. Newfoundland has made many attempts to regain control of this valuable resource, by trying to divert water away from the falls and by requesting that the contract be overturned in court. But in 1984 Canada's Supreme Court ruled in Quebec's favor, upholding the contract, and Newfoundland remains at odds with its neighboring province.

Newfoundland is also in dispute with Canada's federal government about another potential energy source. Scientists believe that the seabed off the coast of Newfoundland contains large reserves of valuable minerals, including oil. One of the largest oil reserves in North America lies in a region under the ocean floor southeast of St. John's. But Canada's Supreme Court ruled that this offshore resource belongs not to Newfoundland but to the federal government. After months of tough negotiations, Newfoundland's provincial government and the federal government signed an agreement that will give Newfoundland a large share of the profits of offshore oil production and some participation in the administration of the project. By 1991, however, construction on the project had not yet begun.

In spite of its economic misfortunes, Newfoundland possesses a remarkable combination of resources and strengths. Perhaps its greatest asset is its proud and hardy people. Newfoundlanders are sure to meet the challenges of the 21st century with their customary integrity and resolve.

The Economy

For centuries, Newfoundland has depended on a single major industry, its fishery. In the second half of the 20th century, efforts have been made to develop other industries and businesses to improve the provincial economy.

Like much of the rest of the modern world, Newfoundland has seen the focus of its economy shift from primary industries, such as forestry and fishing, to the financial and service industries. Today more than 70 percent of Newfoundland's workers are employed in financial and service-related occupations such as banking, real estate, health care, tourism, and communications. Tourism in particular is of growing importance, and the province has undertaken a vigorous campaign to attract visitors to the wide open spaces of Newfoundland and Labrador. Nevertheless, resource-based industries remain important.

The Fishery

Each year, seafood valued at approximately $250 million is harvested from Newfoundland's waters by about 13,000 full-time

Opposite: A Trinity Bay crabber displays his catch. Fishing was the mainstay of the island for centuries and still plays an important role in the economy.
Above: Part of the Churchill Falls hydroelectric plant in Labrador. Energy is one of Newfoundland's most valuable resources, but the province currently receives little of the profit from the electricity produced at this plant.

and 13,000 part-time fishermen. Most of the catch consists of cod, the focus of the fishing industry ever since the Vikings fished in the island's waters a thousand years ago. Atlantic salmon, turbot, haddock, halibut, flounder, herring, lobsters, crabs, and scallops are also caught. Increasingly, less traditional seafoods, such as squid, capelin, and roe, are being harvested for export to Japan and other Asian markets.

Before the advent of large-scale commercial fishing and fish-processing plants, salted and sun-cured cod were exported in large quantities. Today most of the fish is frozen and processed before being sold. This processing adds some $500 million to the value of Newfoundland's catch.

Agriculture

With poor soil and an adverse climate, Newfoundland has never had a significant agricultural output. More than 80 percent of the meat, fruit, and vegetables consumed in the province must be imported. Nevertheless, some farming does occur. Many families have small home gardens that help offset the high cost of store-bought produce, and there are some larger commercial farms. Root vegetables are especially well suited to the province's moist,

Haymaking on the west coast of the island. Newfoundland has little large-scale agriculture, but there is some good pasturage for livestock; in addition, many people tend small vegetable gardens.

cool climate. Potatoes and turnips are the principal crops, and Newfoundland is self-sufficient in turnips. Gardeners usually grow cabbage, beets, lettuce, broccoli, and brussels sprouts as well. Blueberries are the major fruit crop. Newfoundland exports more than 2.2 million pounds (1 million kilograms) of this fruit annually. Smaller quantities of strawberries, cranberries, and apples are also grown.

Farmers in Labrador and on the island tend about 4,400 dairy cows, 1,000 beef cattle, and 1,500 calves every year. In addition, about 16,500 pigs are slaughtered annually, making pork one of the province's few exports. Newfoundland is totally self-sufficient in egg and poultry production.

One potential agricultural resource is reclaimed peat bogs. New developments in land-use technology have made it possible to drain bogland and plant crops in the mineral-rich soil beneath the water. This process, although too expensive to be practical at present, will probably be used in Newfoundland in the future.

Forestry

Newfoundland's forests have been harvested for almost as long as its waters have been fished. European visitors in the 16th and 17th centuries used the province's trees for shipbuilding, for fuel, and for timber to build small fishing villages. Today, approximately 40 percent of the island's area consists of productive forestland, and some logging also takes place in Labrador. The forestry trade employs about 6,000 people in lumber mills, logging camps, and pulp-and-paper plants, mostly on the island. Grand Falls, near the center of the island, is the largest forestry center, although Corner Brook on the west coast is gaining importance.

More than 68 percent of the trees felled in the province are made into newsprint, with an annual value of $300 million. Unfortunately for the people of Newfoundland, the world market for newsprint is notoriously unstable, and this industry is subject to economic slumps. Often the mills close for months at a time while the workers suffer through bitter periods of unemployment.

Another 20 percent or so of Newfoundland's wood is used for fuel. The rest is made into lumber and timber products.

Each year Newfoundland loses a substantial percentage of its potential forest harvest to insects, disease, or forest fires. During the 1970s, the island's forests were severely damaged by an especially lethal infestation of the spruce budworm, an insect that feeds on balsam fir trees. Since then, Newfoundlanders have begun a reforestation program, and they are also trying to develop more efficient and environmentally sound harvesting techniques.

Mining and Energy

Newfoundland island has most of the province's forestry and agricultural resources, but mainland Labrador leads the way in mineral production. The region holds vast stores of iron ore, copper, lead, and zinc.

Iron is the mainstay of Newfoundland's mining industry, accounting for 90 percent of all mineral products exported from the province. Labrador produces more iron ore than any other area in Canada. In recent years, Newfoundland has mined an average of 20 million tons of iron ore each year. Most of the ore is mined around Labrador City and Wabush in western Labrador.

Other mines throughout Labrador produce smaller quantities of metals and industrial minerals. At one time, copper, zinc, and lead were almost as important to the local economy as iron ore. From the 1920s through the 1960s, the Buchans mine in central Labrador produced some of Canada's highest-grade metals. But after decades of concentrated production, most of the accessible minerals have already been taken from Buchans, and current activity at the mine is limited. Metal ores are not the province's only mining products. Gypsum, silica, and limestone are mined in southwest Labrador, and a large asbestos mine on the north shore of Newfoundland island has been in operation since the early 1960s.

Reserves of oil and natural gas have been located off the coast of the province. This energy resource has not yet been developed because the province and Canada's federal government

A mine near Labrador City produces hematite, a type of iron ore. Some of Canada's most extensive mineral reserves are located in Labrador; Labrador City and Wabush are the centers of the mining industry.

Timber from the province's forests lies stacked on the dock at Goose Bay, southern Labrador's main harbor for both military and commercial shipping.

have been disputing ownership of the development rights. Many Newfoundlanders, however, hope that offshore oil drilling will soon provide a much-needed boost to their economy.

Newfoundland has other energy sources as well. The Churchill Falls hydroelectric power plant is the second largest in Canada and one of the largest in the world. Although most of the power produced at Churchill Falls is exported to Quebec, that plant and others along the Churchill River generate enough electricity to make Labrador self-sufficient in energy production. The technology is not yet in place, however, to transport electricity economically from Labrador to Newfoundland island, so energy is more expensive on the island than on the mainland. A large hydroelectric complex and an oil-burning thermal plant have been built on the island as part of an attempt to increase local energy production.

Manufacturing

Most manufacturing in Newfoundland involves processing the province's natural resources. The majority of factories are either pulp-and-paper mills or fish-processing plants. Smaller industries that use local materials include boatbuilding yards, lumber mills, and fruit and vegetable canning operations. In addition, small food-processing plants produce staples such as bread, ice cream, soft drinks, and beer. A large phosphorus plant, a paint-manufacturing factory, and a shipbuilding yard rely on imported materials for their operation.

The People

Life on the Rock, as Newfoundland is fondly known, has never been easy. In the early days of the colony, many settlements were burned to the ground by greedy fishing merchants. People today face different problems—unemployment and a very high cost of living. Despite these hardships, or perhaps because of them, Newfoundlanders have maintained a hardy and independent spirit. Indeed, they are fiercely loyal to their home, acutely aware of its stark beauty, and respectful of its history and enduring culture.

The people of Newfoundland make up one of the most close knit and ethnically homogenous populations in Canada. (Ethnically homogenous means that a high percentage of the people share the same ethnic background.) The majority of Newfoundlanders are of English or Irish descent, and they have proudly preserved many idioms and traditions from the British Isles.

Opposite: Fishermen on Quidi Vidi Lake, near St. John's, prepare to tie up. Many Newfoundlanders are as much at home in a boat as on land; the harbor or riverbank remains the center of many communities.
Above: An Inuit mother and child. Inhabitants of northern Labrador, the Inuit are related to Arctic peoples across Canada and in Siberia.

Visitors to St. John's (pronounced sinJAHNS) and other parts of the Avalon Peninsula will hear a lilting Irish accent. Farther north, the accent is distinctly English, stemming from regions such as Dorset or Devonshire in western England. People throughout the province still use traditional figures of speech, some dating as far back as 300 years. For example, the word *yaffle* means an armful, as in a yaffle of dried fish, and a *kinkhorn* is an Adam's apple. Many of these terms died out long ago in England and Ireland, so English-speaking visitors have a unique opportunity to hear a centuries-old version of their own language.

Although the English and Irish influences dominate the province's culture, there are some important minorities. On the west coast of the island are several small French Canadian fishing villages. Most of the residents are Acadians, descendants of the first French settlers in Canada. Another group of French Newfoundlanders live in western Labrador, near the Quebec border.

Newfoundland also has an active population of Native peoples, both on the island and in Labrador. In recent years, the Micmac people of the island have filed land claims with the federal and provincial authorities, insisting that European settlers took land from their tribes illegally. The Micmac want their tribal territories to be returned to them.

Several thousand Inuits and Innus (Montagnais-Naskapis) still live in Labrador. Most of the Inuit live in the far north, on the frozen tundra that has been their homeland for centuries. Many of them continue to follow the traditional Inuit way of life; others have chosen a more modern course and are involved in the political administration and economic development of northern Canada. Like the Micmac, the Inuit have filed land claims against the federal government.

The Innu live in central Labrador. Many Innu are still trying to maintain their ancestral life-style, hunting caribou in the forests and fishing in the lakes. But the traditional Innu way of life may be threatened by a disturbing intrusion from the 20th century. Low-flying military jets from air bases at Happy Valley–

Goose Bay have upset the caribou herds and other wildlife in the area. The Innu—as well as environmentalists—are concerned that the jets may drive the animals away or even cause their numbers to diminish. The Innu are negotiating this and other issues with Canada's federal government.

Education and Culture

Newfoundland has 600 schools, which accommodate about 140,000 students from kindergarten through 12th grade. The province's first school was established in the 1720s by the Church

Accordionists perform at the Folk Arts Festival in St. John's. This annual event celebrates the traditional music, dance, and crafts of Newfoundland and Labrador. Because of the province's close-knit communities and geographic isolation, folk songs, stories, and customs have been preserved for centuries.

Red Currant Jelly (1972), by Newfoundland artist Mary Pratt, hangs in the National Gallery of Canada in Ottawa.

of England. Since then, the school system has been administered to some extent by the province's various religious denominations. Although the provincial government assumes primary responsibility for the funding of Newfoundland's schools, three different religious committees assist the government in making policy decisions and performing administrative functions. The Roman Catholic Education Committee, the Pentecostal Education Committee, and the Integrated Education Committee—representing the Anglican, Moravian, Presbyterian, Salvation Army, and United Church of Christ populations—together with the provincial Department of Education, make up the Council of Education.

Newfoundland also has several institutions of higher learning. Vocational schools, many of which focus on marine technology and the fishing industry, can be found in Newfoundland's larger towns. The province's only university is Memorial University, founded in 1925. Located on the northern outskirts of St. John's, Memorial is the largest and most respected university in Atlantic Canada. Memorial's second campus, Sir Wilfred Grenfell College, is located in Corner Brook. About 9,800 full-time and 4,000 part-time students are enrolled at Memorial. The university offers degrees in arts and sciences, engineering, medicine, and business administration, but regional concerns are its specialty. The Center for Cold Ocean Resources Research, the Marine Sciences Research Laboratory, and the Maritime Studies Research Institute attract marine biologists and engineers from all over North America.

Memorial University also has the province's Folklore and Language Archives, where students learn about the unique folk traditions established and maintained throughout Newfoundland's history. The very nature of the Newfoundland way of life— cultural homogeneity combined with isolation from the rest of the world—enables folkways to stay alive and meaningful in Newfoundland. As a result, the province is a virtual living laboratory for folk historians from around the world.

Many age-old traditions remain a vital part of the province's cultural life today. One particularly colorful activity, performed by both professional actors and the general population, is called mumming. Dressed in costumes, mummers either perform a traditional folk play or parade through the streets in a procession. At Christmastime, mummers of all ages perform the traditional "house visit," in which small groups of costumed and disguised people visit a neighbor's home. Boisterous and full of fun, the mummers try to fool their hosts, who must try to identify their rowdy guests.

Folk music is an important part of Newfoundland culture. Lively Irish jigs and old English folk songs are heard throughout the province. Newfoundland's best-loved singer and songwriter was Johnny Burke (1851–1931). He wrote hundreds of ballads that celebrated the Newfoundland way of life and recounted events in the history of St. John's. His songs remain popular throughout the province.

The age-old art of storytelling also remains an integral part of the modern Newfoundland cultural scene. Coffeehouses and taverns are often the sites of local storytelling performances. The annual Newfoundland Drama Festival, which was first held in 1950, showcases both professional and amateur storytellers and playwrights from all over the province.

Newfoundland has produced a number of internationally known writers and painters. E. J. Pratt (1883–1964), recognized as one of Canada's finest poets, wrote poems that present realistic and unsentimental looks at maritime life in his native province. One of his most important works was *Newfoundland Verse* (1923).

David Lloyd Blackwood, born in Wesleyville on Bonavista Bay in 1941, is perhaps Newfoundland's best-known visual artist; he is both a printmaker and painter. Blackwood's work reflects the province's unique maritime history, particularly the sea captains of Bonavista Bay. Considered one of Canada's most important etchers, Blackwood now lives in Toronto.

Throughout the province, museums and historical societies have collected impressive displays of irreplaceable artifacts that tell the story of Newfoundland and its people. The Newfoundland Museum in St. John's, for instance, has some of the few relics left by the extinct native Beothuk culture. At L'Anse aux Meadows, a museum depicts the way of life of the ancient Vikings who were the first Europeans to see North America.

Sports and Recreation

The sporting tradition in Newfoundland goes back to the early 19th century. The oldest organized sporting event in North America is St. John's Regatta Day, which has taken place on Quidi Vidi Lake near the capital on the first Wednesday of every August since 1826. Oarsmen from across the province compete in

a 2.5-mile (4-kilometer) race in traditional 6-oared craft. The daylong regatta attracts 50,000 people each year.

Newfoundlanders enjoy a variety of outdoor activities, which also attract tourists who want an active, nature-oriented vacation. Bird-watchers, backpackers, and campers find plenty to do in Newfoundland and Labrador. Sports fishermen flock to the province's lakes and rivers as well as to its seacoasts. Hunters can obtain permits for game on both the island and the mainland. Winter brings ski season. Labrador has some of the best cross-country trails on the east coast of North America, and the Marble Mountain ski resort near Corner Brook on the island is known for its abundant snow and excellent downhill ski trails.

St. John's Regatta Day, a rowing contest, is the oldest sporting event in North America. It has been held since 1826.

The Communities

More than 60 percent of all Newfoundlanders live in towns, mostly in St. John's or other communities on the Avalon Peninsula. A few towns have sprung up in the interiors of both the island and the mainland. Many Newfoundlanders, however, still inhabit the small communities called outports that were founded as the region was originally explored and settled. Outports dot the fringes of both the island and the mainland. Some are as large as towns or villages, others are just a huddle of buildings where a few families live, but all are situated on the coast.

Many outports cannot be reached by road and are accessible only by boat or ship. Set in sheltered inlets to protect them from the harsh Atlantic climate, most Newfoundland outports have at least one church, a school, a store, and a post office. One essential feature of the local landscape is the docks, where fishing boats, small motor launches, and weather-worn rowboats may be seen. The fishery provides the livelihood for most of the outport

Opposite: A Labrador outport. The coasts of the island and the mainland are dotted with these tiny settlements, many of which can be reached only by boat.
Above: The harbor at St. John's, the province's capital.

48

Corner Brook, on the west coast of the island, is the province's second largest city.

residents, and fish-processing plants are located close to many of these communities. After Newfoundland became part of Canada in 1949, government agencies succeeded in closing some of the outports and moving families into the newer towns, where social services and jobs were more readily available. Nevertheless, more than 1,000 outports have survived.

The stark beauty of Newfoundland's cities, towns, and outports is offset by the whimsical charm of their names. Place names such as Come by Chance, Ha Ha Bay, Black Tickle, Heart's Content, Joe Batt's Arm, Witless Bay, and Flower's Cove commemorate episodes in local history, or reflect the relief experienced by early mariners or settlers at having found a safe haven after the rough Atlantic crossing.

St. John's

According to legend, in 1497, on the Roman Catholic holiday called the Feast of St. John the Baptist, explorer John Cabot sailed into the entrance of a snug, protected harbor on the southeast corner of the "new found land" and named the port St. John's in honor of the saint. Fishermen began to use the sheltered bay, and it was not long before a settlement had taken root there. Some historians believe St. John's to be the oldest European settlement in the New World north of Mexico. Today it is both the capital and principal city of the province.

Like Newfoundland itself, St. John's has always looked to the sea for its livelihood. Throughout much of its early history, it was one of the most important ports in eastern Canada. English, French, Basque, and Portuguese fishermen made its magnificent, almost landlocked harbor their haven from the rough and unpredictable Atlantic Ocean. More recently, however, the harbor at St. John's has been overshadowed by other eastern ports, especially Halifax, Nova Scotia. Most goods that come to Newfoundland island from the mainland now arrive by truck, ferried from Nova Scotia to Port aux Basques at the southwestern tip of the island. Nevertheless, the sea remains an integral part of the cityscape.

St. John's is built upon a series of steep hills, which protect the harbor below from high winds and bad weather. The sea is visible from almost every vantage point, especially in the oldest part of the city, where narrow, brightly painted wooden houses line the steep streets. Unfortunately, not much remains of old St. John's because the city was almost completely destroyed by fire several times in the 19th century. The most recent large fire, which left 13,000 people homeless, occurred in 1892. After each fire, the city was painstakingly rebuilt.

Signal Hill, a mass of granite near the mouth of the harbor, offers one of the best views of the city and the harbor. The hill is a natural fortress that has played a significant role in the defense of Newfoundland over the centuries. Every summer, historic battles are reenacted there during a monthlong pageant. At the top of Signal Hill stands Cabot Tower. Built in 1897 to commemorate the 400th anniversary of the discovery of Newfoundland by John Cabot, the tower was the site of an important 20th-century event: the reception of the first trans-Atlantic radio message in 1901 by Italian inventor Guglielmo Marconi.

More than 96,000 people live in St. John's, most of them employed by the federal, provincial, and municipal government agencies that have headquarters in this surprisingly cosmopolitan city. St. John's is also the center of artistic activity in New-foundland. The Newfoundland Symphony Orchestra is based there, and so are a number of theater groups, including CODCO, a repertory company that specializes in character comedy.

CODCO's half-hour comedy show is televised on the Canadian Broadcasting Corporation (CBC) and has garnered the group a following across Canada. Memorial University's Arts and Culture Centre presents performances of Shakespearean plays and other productions. Restaurants, department stores, and nightclubs share the cityscape with parks, office towers, and quaint, old houses. Water Street, thought to be the oldest street in North America, is the center of the shopping district.

Trinity, a seaside hamlet on the island's north coast. Many Newfoundlanders live in small communities such as Trinity, but each year thousands of young people move to the cities or to other provinces in search of better job opportunities.

Corner Brook

Corner Brook, the second largest city in Newfoundland, is located on the opposite side of the island from St. John's. Corner Brook is often called the province's western capital. It is an industrial city of almost 23,000 inhabitants that was formed in 1956 when 4 towns—Curling, Corner Brook West, Corner Brook East, and Townsite—merged.

The forestry trade has been at the center of Corner Brook's growth and development since 1864, when a sawmill opened in the area. In 1923, the Newfoundland Power and Paper Company was formed, and the modern city developed around this large group of resource-related companies. A power plant, located in nearby Deer Lake, has helped to fuel the city's continued economic growth.

In general, the west coast is colder in the winter and warmer in the summer than the east coast. Corner Brook receives more than 150 inches (381 centimeters) of snow every year. This dependable snowfall has led to the development of some excellent ski areas in the Corner Brook region.

Labrador

The mainland portion of Newfoundland is a sparsely populated wilderness speckled with a few industrial towns. Fewer than 30,000 people live in Labrador. Its population may be small, but Labrador has an abundance of natural resources that have made it one of the most hotly contested regions of Canada. Quebec and Newfoundland have been in dispute over the ownership of Labrador for centuries. At present, Newfoundland has the upper hand: The Constitution Act of 1982 confirmed that Labrador was indeed part of Newfoundland.

Labrador's extended seacoast, indented by innumerable fjords, bays, and inlets, has attracted fishermen for nearly a thousand years. Today several ports on the barren, rocky coast provide seasonal docks for ships from Canada, Europe, Japan, and the Soviet Union. But relatively few people are willing to brave the stark winters of Labrador's coastal regions. Red Bay, located on the south coast where the climate is most temperate, has only 300 residents.

The interior of Labrador is far more populous than the coast. At the center of the region is Happy Valley–Goose Bay, a town of about 7,200 people formed when the separate communities of Happy Valley and Goose Bay amalgamated in 1974. During World War II, Goose Bay was the site of the world's largest military airport. Used by the Royal Canadian Air Force, the United States Air Force, and the Canadian Army, the airport employed more than 3,000 Labradorians. The base is currently a refueling and support installation for the air forces of many nations. Surrounded by some of the most beautiful fishing and hunting grounds in North America, Happy Valley–Goose Bay is also the center of Labrador's tourism industry during summer and autumn.

Labador City, an industrial center, and the smaller community of Wabush are located west of Happy Valley–Goose Bay, near the Quebec border. Slightly more than 8,600 people live in Labrador City, making it the largest town on mainland Newfoundland. Most local workers are employed by one of the many iron ore mining plants that have been founded since ore was discovered there in 1892. Labrador City experienced a population boom after 1961, when the Labrador peninsula was linked by railroad with Quebec.

For centuries, Newfoundlanders wrested their living from the sea. Although fishing is no longer central to the province's economy, life still revolves around the sea. Boats are as familiar as cars to many Newfoundlanders.

Things to Do and See

• **Signal Hill National Historic Park and Cabot Tower,** St. John's: Set atop a rocky headland, this park commemorates a number of important events in Newfoundland history, including the arrival of explorer John Cabot in 1497 and the first transatlantic radio transmission in 1901. Breathtaking views of St. John's and the harbor may be enjoyed from Cabot Tower. An interpretive center displays artifacts documenting the city's history.

• **Cape Spear,** 10 miles (16 kilometrs) south of St. John's: This is North America's closest point to Europe and the site of one of Canada's oldest surviving lighthouses, built in 1836.

• **L'Anse aux Meadows:** This UNESCO World Heritage Site is a recreation of the sod village and living quarters built and inhabited by the Vikings in the 10th century A.D.

• **Arts and Culture Centre,** St. John's: The site of the city's main theater, which seats 1,000. The Arts and Culture Centre also includes a large lending library, an art gallery, and several rehearsal rooms.

Opposite: An archaeologist at Port au Choix on Newfoundland's west coast is helping to excavate a several-thousand-year-old settlement of the Dorset, one of Newfoundland's Native peoples.
Above: Once hunted to near extinction, whales now make a different kind of contribution to the provincial economy: They inspire scores of whale-watching tours each year.

• **The Newfoundland Museum,** St. John's: Displays relics of the region's early inhabitants and cultural settlements, including those of the extinct Beothuk people and the Basque whalers. The museum also has artifacts from many of the vessels that have been shipwrecked on Newfoundland's shores.

• **Gander Airport Aviation Exhibition,** Gander: Newfoundland's important role in pioneer aviation, both transatlantic and domestic, is recounted in documents and displays in this small museum located in an airport terminal building.

• **Gros Morne National Park,** 75 miles (120 kilometers) north of Corner Brook: Covering 750 square miles (1,942 square kilometers) of seacoast and mountains, this park has been designated a UNESCO World Heritage Site. It contains sites where archaeologists have uncovered relics of Dorset, Inuit, and Beothuk habitations. It also has rugged hiking trails, facilities for swimming and boating (and surprisingly warm water during the summer), and cross-country ski trails.

• **Terra Nova National Park,** 145 miles (232 kilometers) northwest of St. John's: Canada's easternmost national park, Terra Nova is a naturalist's paradise. The park's starkly beautiful landscape features six lakes carved out by glaciers thousands of years ago. Careful observers may see whales and seals off the shore. Numerous seabirds nest in the region, and animals of many species roam the park.

• **Marble Mountain Ski Resort,** near Corner Brook: Ski runs extend for more than a mile (a kilometer and a half), and drops of about 700 feet (213 meters) make this one of the best ski resorts in Newfoundland.

Tourists in a charter boat cruise past billion-year-old cliffs in Gros Morne National Park.

Festivals & Holidays

Kelligrew's Soiree, Conception Bay: Made famous by folksinger Johnny Burke, this annual festival of eating and merriment is held in July and includes a regatta for the neighboring towns.

Regatta Day, St. John's: Held on the first Wednesday of every August, or "the first fine day thereafter," this is the oldest sporting event in North America. Teams of rowers in racing shells compete on Quidi Vidi Lake. A fair, parade, and festival entertain the more than 50,000 people who attend this annual event.

Newfoundland and Labrador Folk Festival, St. John's: Folksingers and musicians from all over Canada, the United States, and Europe flock to St. John's during August for this international musical celebration of folk traditions.

Winter Carnival, throughout the province: Corner Brook, Mount Pearl, and Labrador City are just few of the Newfoundland communities that host winter carnivals. From January to March, parades, snow-sculpture contests, skiing and skating parties, and other events help to make the province's long winter more enjoyable.

Newfoundland and Labrador Drama Festival, St. John's: Held in mid-April, this event features theater, storytelling, and dance presentations.

Opposite: Each year, battles between the English and the French are reenacted at Signal Hill in St. John's. Cabot Tower, atop the hill, is where Marconi received the first transatlantic radio message.
Above: The Battery, near St. John's, was built by the British army as a coastal defense post during the American War of Independence. During the War of 1812, it protected the colony from a possible U.S. invasion. Today it is a popular—and picturesque—tourist attraction.

Chronology

1000	Vikings build a settlement at L'Anse aux Meadows.
1497	John Cabot sails into the harbor at St. John's.
1610	The West Country Merchants receive control of the Newfoundland fishery.
1713	The Treaty of Utrecht recognizes British sovereignty over Newfoundland.
1811	The British government allows settlement in Newfoundland.
1832	The Newfoundland settlers are permitted to elect an assembly.
1855	Newfoundland is given full colonial status.
1867	Newfoundland decides not to join the new Canadian Confederation.
1892	St. John's is devastated by a huge fire.
1927	Mainland Labrador is awarded to Newfoundland.
1931	The British government recognizes Newfoundland as an independent dominion.
1934	Newfoundland waives its dominion status, becoming a colony once again, and a British-appointed commission takes over its administration.
1949	Newfoundland becomes part of Canada. Joseph R. Smallwood becomes the province's first premier.
1984	The Supreme Court of Canada rules that offshore oil belongs primarily to the federal government.
1989	Newfoundland celebrates its 40th year as a Canadian province.

Further Reading

Armitage, Peter: *The Innu*. New York: Chelsea House, 1991.

Boudreau, Amy. *Story of the Acadians*. Gretna, LA: Pelican, 1971.

Davidson, James W., and Joan Rugge. *Great Heart: The History of a Labrador Adventure*. New York: Viking Penguin, 1988.

Fingard, Judith. *Jack in Port: Sailortowns of Eastern Canada*. Toronto: University of Toronto Press, 1982.

Frideres, James. *Canada's Indians: Contemporary Conflicts*. Englewood Cliffs, NJ: Prentice-Hall, 1974.

Haaland, Lynn. *Acadia Seacoast: A Guidebook for Appreciation*. Edited by Louise Mills and Mercy Johnson. Manset, ME: Oceanus, 1984.

Hocking, Anthony. *Newfoundland*. Toronto and New York: McGraw-Hill Ryerson, 1978.

Holbrook, Sabra. *Canada's Kids*. New York: Atheneum, 1983.

Horwood, Harold A. *Newfoundland*. New York: St. Martin's Press, 1969.

Ingstad, Anne Stine. *The Norse Discovery of America*. Oslo, Norway: University of Oslo Press, 1985.

Law, Kevin. *Canada*. New York: Chelsea House, 1990.

McNaught, Kenneth. *The Penguin History of Canada*. New York: Penguin Books, 1988.

Mowat, Farley. *The Rock Within the Sea: A Heritage Lost*. Boston: Little, Brown, 1969.

Neary, Peter, and Patrick O'Flaherty. *By Great Waters: A Newfoundland and Labrador Anthology*. Toronto: University of Toronto Press, 1974.

Wallis, Wilson Dallam. *The Micmac Indians of Eastern Canada*. Minneapolis: University of Minnesota Press, 1955.

Whiteley, George. *Northern Sea, Hardy Sailors*. New York: Norton, 1982.

Woodcock, George. *The Canadians*. Cambridge: Harvard University Press, 1980.

Index

ACKNOWLEDGMENTS

The Bettmann Archive: p. 20; Diana Blume: p. 6; Canadian Parks Service/J. Steeves:
p. 5; Churchill Falls (Labrador) Corporation: p. 33; Homer Green: pp. 8, 12, 14, 38,
46, 55; Gros Morne National Park, Canadian Parks Service: p. 57; Industry, Science
and Technology Canada photo: pp. 13, 32, 34, 37, 39, 41, 53, 59; Library of
Congress: p. 16; National Archives of Canada: pp. 19 (C38862), 21 (C70648), 22
(NMC-1722); National Gallery of Canada, Ottawa: p. 42; Keith Nicol, Cornerbrook,
Newfoundland: pp. 3, 11, 15, 47, 48–49; Notman Photo Archives, McCord Museum
of Canadian History: p. 25; Courtesy of Provincial Archives of Newfoundland and
Labrador: pp. 26 (NA1578), 28 (B3-174), 29 (B16-155); Reuters/Bettmann Archive:
p. 31; Joe Roman: pp. 36, 54; Debora Smith: p. 7; Wayne Sturge, Department of
Development, Government of Newfoundland and Labrador: p. 45; Michel Thérien:
pp. 9, 58; Courtesy of Tourism Canada, Ottawa: p. 51.

Suzanne LeVert has contributed several volumes to Chelsea House's LET'S DISCOVER CANADA series. She is the author of four previous books for young readers. One of these, *The Sakharov File*, a biography of noted Russian physicist Andrei Sakharov, was selected as a Notable Book by the National Council for the Social Studies. Her other books include *AIDS: In Search of a Killer, The Doubleday Book of Famous Americans*, and *New York*. Ms. LeVert also has extensive experience as an editor, first in children's books at Simon & Schuster, then as associate editor at *Trialogue*, the magazine of the Trilateral Commission, and as senior editor at Save the Children, the international relief and development organization. She lives in Cambridge, Massachusetts.

George Sheppard, General Editor, is a lecturer on Canadian and American history at McMaster University in Hamilton, Ontario. Dr. Sheppard holds an honors B.A. and an M.A. in history from Laurentian University and earned his Ph.D. in Canadian history at McMaster. He has taught Canadian history at Nipissing University in North Bay. His research specialty is the War of 1812, and he has published articles in *Histoire sociale/Social History, Papers of the Bibliographical Society of Canada*, and *Ontario History*. Dr. Sheppard is a native of Timmins, Ontario.

Pierre Berton, Senior Consulting Editor, is the author of 34 books, including *The Mysterious North, Klondike, Great Canadians, The Last Spike, The Great Railway Illustrated, Hollywood's Canada, My Country: The Remarkable Past, The Wild Frontier, The Invasion of Canada, Why We Act Like Canadians, The Klondike Quest*, and *The Arctic Grail*. He has won three Governor General's Awards for creative nonfiction, two National Newspaper Awards, and two ACTRA "Nellies" for broadcasting. He is a Companion of the Order of Canada, a member of the Canadian News Hall of Fame, and holds 12 honorary degrees. Raised in the Yukon, Mr. Berton began his newspaper career in Vancouver. He then became managing editor of *McLean's*, Canada's largest magazine, and subsequently worked for the Canadian Broadcasting Network and the *Toronto Star*. He lives in Kleinburg, Ontario.